The Secret Pet

Written and Illustrated
By Shelley Davidow

Jalmar Press

ISBN 978-1-931061-42-1

Jalmar Press
PO Box 370
Fawnskin, CA 92333
(800) 429-1192
F: (909) 866-2961
www.jalmarpress.com

Dedication

To Drew and Piper

Hannah and Ella

and Lucy

And to Tim, for his inspiration.

About the Author and Illustrator: Shelley Davidow was born and raised in South Africa. She has written numerous books for young and old alike. In 2002, her young adult novel <u>In the Shadow of Inyangani</u> was a finalist in the Macmillan/Picador BBC World Writer's Prize for Africa. Shelley's continued commitment to writing and illustrating phonetic readers is one of her greatest gifts. She lives in Byron Bay, Australia with her husband and son.

About the Phonetic Readers: The first set of six readers, published in 2006, use simple words that the early reader will easily grasp. The words have been carefully chosen by a reading specialist to help students advance from the short vowels, to the silent "e", to the vowel combinations. *The Secret Pet,* is the first chapter book in this series. It's a continuation of the phonetically-based principles that focus on the phonetic vowel teams such as ea, ie, oe, ue, digraphs, open and closed syllables and more.

The story interweaves the animal characters from the first six books into a more in-depth, entertaining and adventurous story. Shelley's ability to create a humorous and thoughtful story is once again shown in this first chapter book. Her beautiful drawings bring the story to life and capture the attention of those early or struggling readers, keeping them reading until they finish the book.

About our Reading Specialist: Mary Spotts has been a remedial reading teacher for over ten years, taking countless classes and seminars to keep current in the field she loves. Her deep understanding that struggling readers still need good stories—even if the books are phonetically based—has been the inspiration in the creation of these books. Mary has been a constant guide, ensuring that the books address specific phonetic principles while retaining a gently humorous story line.

Dear Boys and Girls,

I hope you enjoy this story of a boy and his magical pet, Jake. In real life, of course, you should always remember that wild animals are WILD! Keep a safe, respectful distance from snakes and don't ever try to catch one or handle one!

Shelley Davidow

Table of Contents/Phonetic Concepts

Chapter One: **A Secret**   **1**
(ea, as in *treat*)

Chapter Two: **The Rescue**   **13**
(ie, as in *pie*; oe as in *toe*)
(ue, as in *blue*)

Chapter Three: **A Snake at School**   **25**
(ch, *chip*; sh, *ship*; th, *thin*, *then*)
(wh, *wheel*)

Chapter Four: **Jake, Sam, and Ned**   **37**
(ore, as in *more*; are, as in *care*)

Chapter Five: **Mr. Chen's Snake Book**   **49**
(ff, ll, ss as in fell, huff, hiss. — one-syllable
words ending with double consonants
after a short vowel)

Chapter Six: **A Ring in the Sand**   **59**
(ing, as in *thing*; ink as in *think*)

Chapter Seven: **Jake the Spy**   **69**
(short words ending with a long vowel,
as in *me, be, so, go, no*)
(y, as in *my, by*)

Chapter Eight: **A Big Fright**   **81**
(ind, as in *kind*; old, as in *cold*; ild, as in *wild*;
ost, as in *most*; igh family words, as in *knight, fight*)

Chapter Nine: **The Snatch-Attack**   **93**
(ck, as in *rock*; tch, as in *snatch*; dge, as in *hedge*)

Chapter One: A Secret

"No more pets this year!" said Tim's mom. "You have Sam Cat and Ned Dog. They eat a lot and make a lot of mess."

"Please, Mom, can I keep this snail?" said Tim. "Her name is Kay, and she likes me."

"Snails like to be in the sun and the rain. They do not like to be inside a box."

Tim was sad, but he took his snail
box outside and let Kay go. She was

glad. She liked
the sun and the
wind from the

sea. She liked the big sky.

The next day Tim got on his bike
and rode to the beach near his home.
To get to the beach, he had to cross a
stream. Tim felt the heat. He had a
rest by the stream. Then he saw a
long, black streak slide under a leaf. It
was a snake. The snake came out from
under the leaf. Tim did not want to
breathe.

"I am not afraid of a snake!" he said. "I like snakes a lot."

"Did I hear you say that you like snakes a lot?"

Tim looked at the snake. The snake looked at Tim.

 "Can you speak?" said Tim.

"Yessssss!" said the snake.

"What's your name?"

"My name is Jake," said the snake.

"Please to meet you, Jake. My name is Tim. Come with me to the beach to see the sea."

The sky was clear. Tim rode to the beach, and Jake slid to the beach. The sea was teal and green. The sun was hot, and Jake hid in the shade of a dune. Tim made a heap of sand into a seat. He sat on his seat, and Jake slid onto Tim's feet.

"Will you be my pet?" said Tim.

"What is a pet?" said Jake.

"If you will be my pet, I will take you home. I will give you a feast of things to eat. I will give you ice cream and green peas and brown wheat, bread and meat, and you will love it. You can sleep near me in my room. You can play with me and even go to school with me."

Jake had never eaten ice cream or green peas or brown wheat bread. He had never slept in a room. He lived in a deep, cool hole, and he ate snake food.

Jake looked at Tim. He was a nice boy. He was not afraid of Jake, and Jake was not afraid of him.

"If you teach me, I will be your pet," said Jake.

"I will have to sneak you into my home," said Tim. "My mom said no more pets this year."

"Will she scream if she sees me?" said Jake.

"No. She will not scream, but she will leap up, and then she will make me let you go."

"I want to be your pet," said Jake. "I want to sneak into your home. It will be fun."

It was Tim's dream to have a snake as a pet. Tim and Jake sat as the sun sank to the sea at the end of the day. Then Tim got on his bike. Jake slid in the sand.

They made their way from the sea to the stream. At the stream they had a drink. Then Jake let Tim pick him up. Tim put Jake the black snake around his neck. Tim and Jake were a team.

Tim went softly to his neat room. He could hear his mom say, "Time to eat!"

Tim put Jake into his shirt. While he ate, he fed Jake at the same time. He fed Jake a bean, but Jake did not like it. He let it fall on the floor. Then Tim fed him a pea. Jake did not like the pea. He let that fall on the floor too. Then Tim fed him some meat. He liked the meat, and he ate it.

After a while Jake began to squeak. It was very soft, but Tim could hear it. It was time to go to his room.

"May I please leave?" said Tim.

"Yes, you may, but please clean up that pea and that bean," said his mom. Tim bent down and got the pea and bean. Jake was just a big crease in Tim's shirt. They went up to Tim's room.

Tim got his snail box. It was a good bed for a snake. The box had a lid. Jake slid underneath the lid and went to sleep.

Tim went to sleep too. His dream was real. He had a secret pet snake in a box by his bed. The snake could speak. Tim could teach Jake the Snake tricks and how to go on a leash. He would take Jake to school and teach him to read.

Chapter Two: The Rescue

When the sun came up on Tuesday, Tim did not want to lie in bed so he sat up. Jake spied Tim from his box.

"How did you ssssleep?" hissed Jake from the box.

"I slept well, thank you," said Tim. He was full of joy. He stuck his toes into the air. Then he got out of bed. Jake slid out of the box.

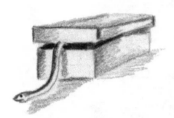

"Just wait," said Tim. "I need to brush my teeth."

Tim went on tiptoe out of the room. Jake slid along the soft, blue rug out of the room. Then Jake saw Tim's mom and slid into a new room. He saw a big, empty box and he slid into a big, round hole in the box. It was shiny and cool inside. There were lots of tiny holes too. Jake did not have a clue what kind of box this was.

Tim's mom came into the 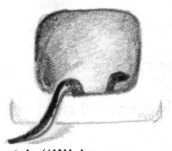 room. "Tim," she said, "I'll have your shirt dried soon!"

She took a wet shirt and put it into the funny box. She did not see the snake. Then she put a tissue into the box. Jake was under the shirt and the tissue. Tim's mom closed the box. Jake and the shirt lay inside.

Then Jake felt a bump! The box began to spin and spin! Jake and the shirt and the tissue went round and round! They went up. They went down. Then they went upside down!

Jake was tied to the shirt. The shirt was tied to Jake. He tried to stop going round and round and upside down, but he could not stop. The box spun all by itself! Then the box got hot. The shirt had dried. Jake was fried!

"Where are you, Jake?" Tim  cried. He opened the funny box and saw Jake tied to the shirt and the tissue.

"Oh Jake the Snake, you almost died!"

Tim came to the rescue. He got Jake and the shirt and the tissue out of the box.

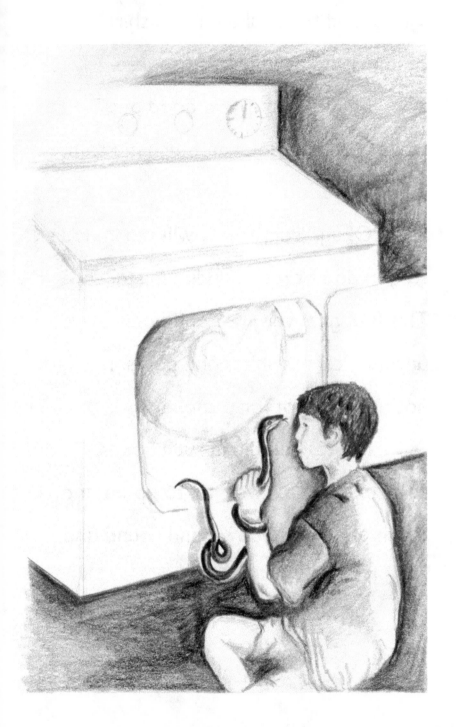

Tim untied the snake and his shirt. Jake was hot and glad to be free.

"Maybe I am not a good pet," said Jake. "But you can teach me to be a good pet."

"Okay," said Tim. "I will teach you, so you do not make undue mistakes. This box gets very hot and goes around. It dries shirts and pants. It is not a good spot for a snake."

"Snakes can die in such boxes," said Jake. "But it was fun to go up and down and upside down and round and round!"

Tim put on his shirt. He put Jake around his neck, under his shirt. They went to eat. Tim sat with his mom and his dad. They ate toast and jam and some apple pie. Tim's mom said, "Has your shirt dried, Tim?"

"Yes," he said.

"Will you have a bit more pie?" said Tim's dad.

"Yes, please," said Tim. He took a bit of pie and gave it to Jake under his shirt.

"Do you have pie down your shirt?" said his dad.

"No," Tim said. It was no lie. Jake ate that bit of pie.

On the way to school, Tim said to Jake, "Do you like apple pie?"

"I like apple pie," said Jake. "If I like apple pie, am I a good pet?"

"You are a very good pet," said Tim to the snake around his neck. "We just have to make you a very safe pet. I do not want you to get hurt."

"What is a school?" said Jake.

"I will show you."

"Can you swim in a school?" said Jake.

"No, but you can swim in a pool," said Tim. "Kids go to school to read books."

"Can I read a book?" said Jake.

"I could teach you to read," said Tim.

"Would kids be afraid of me?" said Jake.

"Yes. There are kids who are afraid of snakes," said Tim.

"I do not bite," said Jake. "And I will not pursue the kids. I will be a secret pet. I will lie around your neck. I will not go into funny boxes. Tell me what I should do."

Tim kept Jake around his neck. Jake was like a black tie on the inside of a shirt.

Tim told Jake what to do, and what NOT to do at school:

"1. Do not let the teacher see you.

2. Do not play with glue. That stuff will stick to you.

3. Do not go far away, or you may get lost.

4. Do not play with tape. It also sticks to you like glue.

5. You can read books with me when I read.

6. You can sleep in my backpack or my pocket or my desk.

7. You can play with the kids, if I tell them to be good.

You are the best pet, Jake."

When Tim said that, it was Jake's cue. He would be good at school. He would not argue with the teacher or pursue the kids. He had been rescued, and he was glad.

Chapter Three: A Snake at School

Tim sat at his desk. He lifted the lid of the desk just an inch to check on Jake. He was awake. Jake was just like a black rope next to a bunch of Tim's pens. It was such fun to have a snake at school. Tim had to wait to chat with Jake.

"Tim, please close the lid of your desk," said Mr. Chen. "It's time to read."

All the kids got books out and began to read. Jake wanted to read. When Mr. Chen looked away, Tim lifted the lid of the desk just an inch to let Jake see his book.

Jake slid his thin neck out of the desk. "Shhhhh," whispered Tim.

But Jake did not want to stay in the desk. He saw the blue sky outside and felt a rush of joy. He shot out of the desk, onto Tim's lap, and across the room. Tim saw a thin, black thing flash across the floor.

"Where are you going, Jake?" Tim whispered.

"What did you say?" said Mr. Chen.

"Nothing," said Tim.

"Would you like to read to me?" said Mr. Chen. Tim went to read to Mr. Chen. He looked for Jake by the trash can, but he could not see him. Tim wished he could go out and chase after Jake.

While Tim read, Jake slid outside. He saw the shade of a

big bush. That was much better than the shade of a desk. Jake slid onto the smooth sand. It was such a fresh, fun day. Jake slid up the bush and lay on a branch.

Tim and all the kids ran out to play. Lots of feet came thumping like thunder near the bush. Tim saw the shade. He said, "I think Jake loves the shade."

"Jake!" he cried. "Jake! Where are you?"

"Who is Jake?" said the kids.

Then something black whizzed out of

the bush in a

rush.

"Jake!"

yelled Tim in a

shrill way. "Please come back!"

"A snake!" shouted the kids.

In a flash, they dashed after the
thin, smooth shape that went shooting
down the path. Tim did not stop. It
was a thrill for Jake to rush from this
bush to that bush. School was so much
fun! The kids could not catch Jake. The
shade was black, and so was Jake. He
hid in the shade of a bush with white

blossoms. The blossoms were sweet.

Tim smashed into the white bush with

a crash. He gave

a cheer.

"There you
are, Jake! Watch
out for that bunch
of kids."

"Those kids
like snakes," said Jake. "I want to meet
them."

Jake let Tim catch him and hold
him next to his chin. When the kids
came up to Tim, they all began to
chat.

"Why do you have a pet snake?"

"Can I hold him?"

"Will he bite?"

Tim said, "This is Jake. He will not bite. You can each hold him for a bit."

It was a thrill for the kids to hold the thin, black snake. Jake did not speak to the kids. He sat on their hands and lay around their necks.

"This is my secret pet," said Tim. "Do not tell Mr. Chen. Do not  tell my mother. If you keep him a secret, you can play with him."

"We will keep him a secret," said the kids. They gave Jake back. Tim let

Jake lie around his neck under his chin. Jake was just a shape under a shirt. The kids and Jake went back to class.

"Why did you rush out to the bush?" whispered Tim to Jake.

"I love shade," said Jake. He saw that Tim was sad.

"I do not want you to get lost," said Tim. "I want you to be my pet."

"Yes," said Jake. "But pet snakes like the shade of a big bush."

"Yes, they do" said Tim. "Pet snakes need bushes and branches and things. You are not a desk snake."

"But I do like school and the kids. I like to read too. I think I'd like to read in the shade of a bush."

In class Tim got a book about snakes. Jake sat in his shirt. He saw a green snake and a brown snake in the book.

"Which snake looks like me?" Jake said.

"This black one looks like you," Tim said. "The book says: 'This snake likes shade and will not bite.'"

"Yessss!" hissed Jake. "That is me! Now I can read it too, see? 'This snake likes shade and will not bite.'"

"That's very good, Jake."

On the way home, Jake said, "I think school is good. Can I be a secret school pet?"

"Yes," said Tim. "And I will not stop you if you need to dash out into the shade. I will find snake books for you to read. I will let you play with the kids." When they got home, Jake slid into the snail box that was his snake box now and went to sleep.

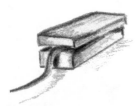

Chapter Four: Jake, Sam, and Ned

It was the weekend, and Tim was still asleep. Sam Cat liked to sleep on Tim's bed. He got up and saw the snail box on the blue carpet. He heard a scratch in the box. He did not see that the box was a snake box.

Jake slid out of the box. "Sorry," he said when he saw the cat. "Did I wake you?"

Sam Cat did not care to speak with black snakes in snail boxes. He gave Jake a very hard stare. He did not want to share the room with him.

Snakes did not sleep in rooms. They slept in bushes outside. Rooms were for boys and for soft, sweet cats like Sam.

"Sssso," said Jake. "I am Jake. You must be Sam. Tim said he had a cat. I am a pet too. We will have to share Tim."

Sam Cat's stare said BEWARE, but that did not scare Jake!

Sam got off the bed. Jake slid to Sam and rose up. The snake was as tall as the cat!

Sam bared his teeth. He hissed like a snake, and Jake hissed back. Sam's ears went flat. Jake said, "Yes, you were here before me, but now I am Tim's pet."

Sam Cat put up his paw. Jake the Snake lifted his tail. Sam gave Jake a slap. Jake's tail shot out to tweak Sam's ear.

Tim woke up.

"Please keep score," said Jake to Tim. "One point to the cat and one to the snake."

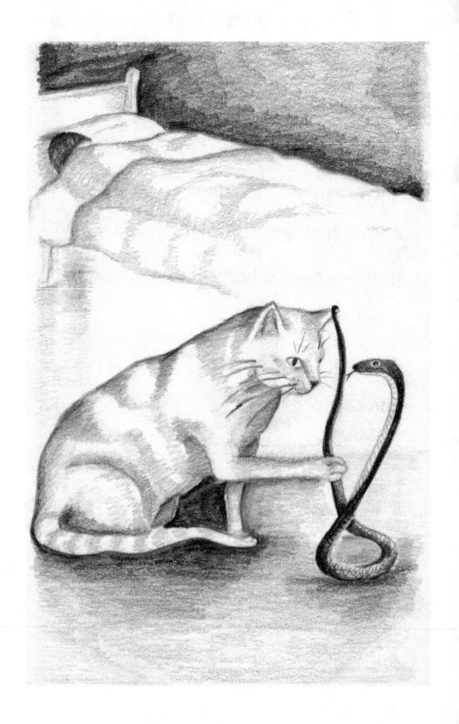

Tim did not want to see more. "Stop this, please. You are both my pets, Sam and Jake!"

But there was more. "Two points to the cat and two to the snake. Now three to the snake," said Jake. "Two slaps for the snake and three tweaks for the cat."

 "No more," Tim said. "This makes me sore. You are both my pets."

Sam did not scare Jake, and Jake did not scare Sam. Tim said, "The score is even. I like you both the same, okay?"

Sam Cat did not care for more. He licked his fur. Sam wore himself out. Jake was a bore.

Sam Cat went to Tim's parent's room and got on the bed. Jake slid after Sam. Tim had to follow his snake and his cat.

Sam sat on the bed and gave Jake a good stare. Sam was not a mean cat. Jake was not a mean snake. Tim took Jake and put him around his neck. He went out of his mom and dad's room and out of his house.

It was morning, and the sun was in the sky. Tim took a look and saw Sam follow him. There in the sun lay Ned Dog. When Sam saw Ned, he ran to play with the dog. Tim put Jake on the sand in the shade. Ned saw Jake.

"My pets should all be friends," said Tim. Ned Dog came to sniff Jake. Jake stood up tall and thin and black. Then Sam Cat came to sit next to Ned. His ears were flat on his head.

"Yessss," said Jake. "I am a good pet. I want to be friends with a cat and a dog."

Ned slowly sat down next to Jake. Sam came to sit next to Ned. Jake slid up  to Ned and onto his paw. It did not scare Ned Dog to have a snake on his bare paw. Sam Cat lay down in the sand next to Ned and Jake. His ears were not flat.

"It is rare that a snake and a dog and a cat can all be friends," said Tim. "It is rare that a boy can have a secret pet snake and keep him in his room."

Ned and Tim and Sam began to run. They ran from the house to the sea. Jake could follow. He was fast. They all went to the stream and then the shore.

The sea was big and blue. Sam Cat saw that Jake was not a bore. Jake could make a big 'S' in the sand with his shape.  Ned could chase Jake, but he could not catch him. The pets could share Tim.

"Let's play Hide and Seek," said Tim. "Jake, you and Sam and Ned can hide. I will come and find you."

"Okay," said Jake. "Please count to ten."

Tim counted to ten. He did not peek. Then he went to find his pets. He saw Sam in the shade of a bush on the shore and Ned behind a sand dune. But

Tim could not find Jake. Tim and Ned and Sam ran this way and that way.

"Which way did he go?" said Tim. Ned ran along the shore to sniff the sand and find the snake trail. Sam was with Tim.

"Look!" cried Tim. Jake lay on the shore just like a long, black bit of seaweed.

"I am a good seaweed snake," said Jake. He was full of sand. Ned began to leap up on Tim. He was full of joy. Sam began to purr next to Tim.

Then the snake and the dog and the cat and the boy went away from the seashore. They had to follow the path to the stream. After that they had to follow the path back to their home.

Chapter Five: Mr. Chen's Snake Book

Jake had learned some tricks. He could make an 'S' in the sand. He could tweak a cat's ear with his tail. He could begin to read a snake book. Jake was a good pet.

Tim kept his secret well. He did not tell his mom or his dad about Jake.

At school, Jake did not hiss or make a fuss. He lay on the bookshelf on top of the snake book. Jake wanted to learn to spell. He sat still on the

snake book and said, "Snake —
S.N.A.K.E. — that's me!"

Mr. Chen said to the class,
"Today I am going to tell you about
snakes. Some

snakes are

big, and

some are

small. Some

snakes bite,

and you can

swell up and get sick

or even die from the bite. But most

snakes are safe if you do not play with

them."

"Do you like snakes?" said Tim.

"Yes, I like snakes," said Mr. Chen. He went to get a book on snakes but did not see Jake. When Mr. Chen took the book on snakes, Jake stood up tall on the book. Mr. Chen saw the snake! He let go of the book and gave a yell.

The book fell. Tim saw Jake fall. Jake slid to the wall. "A snake came out of a book on snakes!" cried Mr. Chen. Jake slid out of the room and went down the hall. Tim heard a shout fill the room. There was a big fuss. Mr. Chen had to huff and puff and sniff. He

could not stand still. Tim saw him
press his lips together.

"What a snake!" Mr. Chen said.

"Can I go and see that snake?"
said Tim. "I can tell if it is a safe snake
or not. I like snakes a lot."

"I can tell that you like snakes,"
said Mr. Chen. I like snakes too. You
may go and see if you can find that
snake."

The kids
wanted to go with
Tim, but Mr. Chen
said. "When the

bell rings, you can all go out. But Tim
can leave the class now to find the
snake."

The kids saw
Tim go down the
hall and onto the
grass. Tim did not
make a fuss. He did

not stress. He ran up a hill and gave a
call: "Jake! J.A.K.E. the Snake,
S.N.A.K.E. Can you spell? Can you
tell I need to get you back?"

Tim fell on some moss on the hill.
There was a hiss.

Jake the Snake said, "What a
fuss! What a yell!"

"Mr. Chen likes snakes," said Tim. "He was afraid just for a second."

Tim took Jake and hid him in his shirt. "Good trick, Jake," Tim said. "But how am I to keep you a secret now?"

"Just don't tell," said Jake.

"Okay," said Tim. He ran across the grass and down the hall and back to the class.

"Well?" said Mr. Chen. He did not see the small swell around Tim's neck.

"Well, that snake we saw is a safe snake," said Tim. This was not a lie. "He will not bite. He likes hills and grass and cliffs, and he likes kids too."

"Maybe we will see him again," said Mr. Chen.

"Maybe we will," said Tim.

"That would be fun," said the kids. They did not look at Tim. His secret was a class secret now, and they all had to keep it. Jake had to keep his head far under Tim's shirt.

Mr. Chen got the book on snakes off the ground. He read it to the class. He also said, "Do not drop the book on snakes, and do not make a fuss."

Tim smiled. The kids smiled.

"So," said Jake to Tim after class. "It's a good thing I am still a secret. I hope the kids will not tell your mother or Mr. Chen."

"They will keep the secret," said Tim. He had Jake on his arm. They went across the grass. When

they got home, Sam Cat was sitting in front of the house. Sam saw Tim and Jake. Tim put his finger to his lips. "Shhhh," he said. "Do not tell!"

Then Ned Dog came up to Tim and Jake and began to lick Tim's leg. "Shhhh," said Tim. "You must keep the secret, Ned."

Sam and Ned would not tell Tim's mom. They could not speak. But Jake was a secret pet who could speak. Jake was glad because he went to school and because he could read. Well, at least he could read one snake book!

Chapter Six: A Ring in the Sand

Tim was at the beach with his mom and dad. It was a hot spring day, but Tim would not take off his shirt.

"Why do you have your shirt on?" said his dad.

"The sun is too hot for me," said Tim. It was no lie. The sun was hot. But Tim had his shirt on because Jake was around his neck. Tim put his feet in the sea. He had to blink in the sun.

"Come for a swim," said his dad.

"The salt makes my eyes sting," said Tim. So his dad went for a swim.

Then Tim heard his mom shout, "Oh NO!" Tim ran to her. "Oh, Tim," she said, "I lost the ring that your Dad gave me."

"Where did it fall?" Tim asked.

"I took it off for a second to dust off the sand. I think it fell down here."

Tim and his mom could not find the ring. She said, "I think I saw it sink into the sand over here." Tim wanted to find the ring. He had to think a lot how to do that.

He said, "Mom, I need a drink. Did we bring things to drink?"

"Yes, we did bring drinks," said his mom. "Wait here and see if you can find the ring. I'll go and get our drinks."

As soon as Tim's mom was on her way to get drinks, Tim took Jake out of his shirt. Tim's dad was

 swimming far out in the sea. He was king of the sea. "Jake," said Tim, "do

you think you could slink under the sand and find the ring?"

"I think I could swing it," said Jake. "I will slink under the sand like a bit of string and see if I can find the ring and bring it back."

Tim swung Jake down onto the sand. Jake was strong. He began to make himself very long and thin, like a string.

Tim saw Jake's head sink into the sand, and then he could not see the snake. Jake took a long time.

Tim's mom was on her way back with drinks.

"Is anything wrong?" Tim said softly. He still could not see Jake.

Jake did not come up. Tim saw his dad far out in the sea. Tim swung his foot in the sand, and then he saw Jake. The snake had a gold thing on his fang.

Tim's mom came back. "A drink for you," she said.

"Thank you."

"No luck with my ring?" his mom said. Jake lay next to a long bit of black seaweed on the sand. They were the same color.

Tim's mom did not see the black snake. Jake let the gold ring drop onto the sand. Tim saw the ring wink and blink in the sun. Tim sprang onto the ring. He was so glad that he could have sung.

"Mom! Look!" Tim took the ring and dusted off the sand.

"Tim, is that my ring?"

"Yes. It was in the sand."

"Oh, thank you!" said his mom. She was so glad to have her ring

back. She gave Tim a big hug. Then
she took the ring and put it back on
her finger.

Tim gave Jake a
wink. His secret
pet snake lay
on the beach
like seaweed.
He was as
black as ink. When Tim's dad came
back from the sea and got out, Jake
had to shrink back.

　　Tim's mom said, "I lost my ring in
the sand. I clung to the hope that I
could find it. Then, what a thing! Tim
found it! I'm so glad!"

Tim's dad gave him a hug. Tim wanted to tell his mom and dad that Jake the Snake had to slink under the sand to get the ring. He could not think of what to say, so he just hung his head.

Tim's mom sang. She was full of joy. Tim's dad swung his shirt over his back and said, "Time to go!" They went along the beach.

Tim saw Jake in the sun. He had time to reach down and get the long, black, fake-seaweed snake and hang him around his neck.

"How did you find that ring?" Tim said.

"Not an easy thing," said Jake. "Sand makes snake eyes sting. I had to make myself long and strong to slink along in the soft sand. But rings can sing songs. I heard a clink and a chink in the sand."

"Jake, I think you are such a good pet. If my mom could see that you got her ring, she would let me keep you as a pet."

"Then I would not be a secret pet," said Jake.

"That's true," said Tim.

Chapter Seven: Jake the Spy

The next day, the sky was blue, the sun was hot, and Tim's dad was in the yard.

"Oh, no!" he said. "Look at all the holes in the yard!"

Tim ran out the back door, his secret pet around his neck. The yard was full of holes!

"Tim, did you see who made these holes?"

"No," said Tim.

"Do you think they look like snake holes?"

Tim said, "I think they are too big."

"What could they be?" Tim bent down and put his nose to a hole. It was damp and cool in there. Jake had to peek at the hole too.

"Shhh," said Tim.

"We must try to find out who made these holes," said Tim's dad.

"If you trust me, I will find out who made these holes, and then I will fix them," Tim said.

"That would be so good," said Tim's dad. "It will make my work easy."

"By tomorrow there will be no more holes," said Tim. He went back inside with his secret pet.

"Okay, Jake. What do you think?"

"Did you see the dry heaps of sand by the holes?" said Jake.

"Yes," said Tim.

"We snakes don't do that. When you are asleep, I will be a spy. I will go into the holes and try to find out who made them. Then I will stop them."

"That's good work, Jake the Spy. Then I can fix the holes, and my dad will be glad."

When it got dark, Tim went to sleep. The big, white moon came out. Jake the Spy slid out of the room and under the door. He felt the cool wind on his back.

As soon as he got to the first hole, he could smell the damp earth. He also could hear something.

Jake the Spy slid into the hole to pry.

A Spy must pry. It is his job!

He could hear tiny feet go by.
Then he felt a nose on his nose.

"My, my!" said the nose. "At last.
My wife sent me to find you, Jake the
Snake. We thought we would never
see you ever again."

"Mike the Mole?" said Jake.

"Yes, yes," said Mike.

"You thought I was lost?" said
Jake.

"My wife
and I thought
you were lost or
eaten! Where

have you been?"

"I am a pet," said Jake. "I am Tim's secret pet now."

"You cannot be a pet," said Mike. "You must go free. We are wild. We are not pets, Jake. We do not live with boys or girls or moms or dads. We bite. They do not like us."

"I do not bite. Tim likes me," said Jake. "And I like Tim."

"Okay," said Mike. "I am so glad that you are glad. It took me a long

 time to find you. I had to ask a slug, a bug, a snail, a cat, and a dog.

Cats and dogs like moles…to EAT! It was very hard."

"You are a good mole, Mike," said Jake. "I like you. Snakes do not always like moles, but I like you. Long ago I did not like moles. Then you put your nose into my home. The cat and the dog will like you too. They like me now. You could be a pet, Mike."

"No thank you!" said Mike. "I would not even try my luck. I am a free mole. And I bite."

"So why are there mole holes all over the yard?" said Jake.

"That is my trail," said Mike. "I had to try to find you. My wife said she would fry me if I did not find you."

"Say 'Hi' to your wife. I will try to come and see you sometime."

"She will like that," said Mike. "Sorry about the holes."

"We will fix them," said Jake.

Mike the Mole left Jake the Spying Snake and went back to his wife to tell her the story.

Jake the Spy slid back under the door into Tim's room. Then he slid into his box and went to sleep.

When the moon went down, and the sun came up, Tim woke.

"What did you find, Jake the Spy?"

Jake told Tim about Mike the Mole.

"I like that story," said Tim. "Let's go fix the yard."

So Tim and Jake went out into the yard. Tim put the sand back into the holes, and Jake slid over them to make them flat. A fly came by, and

Jake got the fly and ate it fast. "Snack," said Jake. Tim smiled.

When Tim's dad got up, he came outside. Tim had to get Jake under his shirt fast.

"Wow!" said Tim's dad. "Look at that yard. How did you do it?"

"A mole made the holes," said Tim. "And Dad, we…uh, I …I can say that he will not do it again."

Tim's dad smiled. "So you and the mole made that deal?"

"Um, kind of." Jake the Spy lay flat between his shirt and his skin.

Chapter Eight: A Big Fright

Tim's best toy was a knight. The knight was made of wood. Sometimes Tim would play wild games with the knight. He had a story for the knight. Today, in the story, he made the knight fight an old dragon.

"Jake, will you be the dragon?" Tim said.

Jake was in his cool box. "I had a good nap," he said. "So, yesss, I will be a dragon. I will fight your knight and

protect my gold. Then I will hold the
knight high, and he will be in a plight."

"How will the knight get out of
his plight?" said Tim

"He will be told
to leave my gold and
to let me grow old in
my dragon cave. I will
almost eat him, but after he has had a
fright, I will let him go."

"Yes!" cried Tim. "I like that a lot.
The box is your cave, Dragon. This is
your gold. Go in and hide. Here comes
the knight to find you. He has you in
his sight!"

Tim had to hold the knight. He came at the black dragon. The dragon stood on his tail and got the knight.

Jake held the knight up high. Tim went to jump on his bed. It was so much fun to see his knight with a real dragon.

"A dragon fight!" he cried. The dragon went wild. He had the knight tight.

"What a plight! Help! Help!" Tim cried for his knight who could not speak.

Then Tim's mom came into his room. "What's the matter, Tim?"

She went white with fright. What a sight! There, in bright daylight, was a long, black snake in Tim's room, with Tim's toy.

"Eeeeeeek!" yelled Tim's mom. "A snake! A cold, wild snake in the room with my child. Help!"

Tim got off his bed. Jake let go of the knight. Tim went to pick Jake up and hold him. He  thought his mom might faint with fright.

Tim gave a sigh. The dragon fight was over. "Mom, this is Jake.

He's my secret pet snake. But now I
have no more secrets. He's not wild,
he's tame. He plays games with me,
and he will not mind if you hold him."

"He might bite," said his mom. "I
got such a fright to see you with a big,
black snake in your room. I told you,
Tim, no more pets. No snakes in this
home."

"But Mom, Jake is a good pet.
He's much better than most pets. He
will not bite or make a mess. He is a
good snake."

"Yes," said Tim's mom. "I can see
he is a good snake. But snakes are

wild. They need to be out in the wild. You will have to let him go."

Jake did not speak. Tim said, "Let him stay just one more night."

"Okay. Let me ask your dad," said his mom.

Now Tim was in a plight. He did not want to let Jake go. He held him tight.

"Your mom is right," said Jake. "I am a 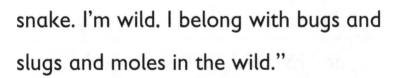 snake. I'm wild. I belong with bugs and slugs and moles in the wild."

"No you don't!" said Tim. You belong with cats and dogs and pets.

You can eat what we eat, and you can read, and you can find things and play games. You are the best pet!"

"Thank you," said Jake. "Yes, it's true that I do like to be a pet. But if your mom and dad say that I must go, then I must go. I am not a secret pet now."

Tim was so sad. He could not let Jake go. He was very sad about the knight and the fight. If only he had not been so wild.

Jake was sad too. He was a good pet, and he liked his box in Tim's room. He liked to play games and go to school. He liked to help find rings

and spy on moles at night. This was a
good life.

When it was time to eat, Tim
took Jake on his arm to meet his dad.
Sam Cat sat on the floor. Tim let Jake
down. Jake and Sam went nose to
nose.

"Sam seems to like that snake!"
said Tim's dad.

"Right, Dad. Sam likes Jake."

Ned Dog lay by the door. Jake
went to Ned and slid right onto him.

Ned lifted his head and went nose to nose with Jake.

"What a sight! Ned seems to like Jake too!" said Tim's dad. Tim's mom said, "Okay. Let's eat. What does Jake like?"

Jake ate with Tim and his mom and his dad. He was around Tim's arm. They ate meat, and Jake ate that too. They ate chips and beans and  peas. Jake did not like beans and peas. Both Tim's mom and his dad were kind to Jake, but they would not hold him.

"I have never had dinner with a snake," said Tim's dad.

"He's the best snake," said Tim. "I want him to stay."

Tim's Dad was sad. "I can see that," he said. "But your mom is right. Your snake is wild, and he must go back into the wild. He can stay just for the night."

Chapter Nine: The Snatch-Attack

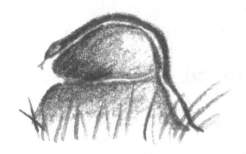

The next day Tim took his snake out into the back yard. His mom and dad came out too.

"It's time to let him go, " said Tim's dad.

Tim looked up into the sky. Then he looked at the snake. "I will miss you very much, Jake."

Tim went with Jake to the hedge at the edge of the yard. There was a rock with a ledge next to the hedge. "I will stay and watch you go. Come back and visit me sometime."

Tim was sad. Even his mom and dad were sad. Tim let Jake go.

"Ssssso long. I'll ssssseee you," hissed Jake. He slid onto the ledge on the rock. Then he slid into a ditch under the hedge.

"Did that snake just say that sentence?" said Tim's dad.

"Yes he did," said Tim. "Jake speaks. He also brings good luck. He went under the sand to get Mom's ring when it was lost. Then he went as a spy to solve the riddle of who made the holes in the yard. And now he may never come back."

Just then a big blue heron struck the ledge of the rock with her long beak. Tim and his mom and dad could see that this was an attack. The beak went 'click' and 'crack' on the rock. Then they got a shock. The big blue heron had Jake in her beak! He was stuck. Tim's mom took a stick and ran at the heron.

"You let go of that snake right now!" Tim's mom cried as she struck the heron on the beak. "That is our snake. You may not snatch him! Give him back!"

The heron opened her beak to peck Tim's mom, and Jake fell out! Tim's mom ran to pick him up. Then the heron beat her big wings, and Tim's mom had to duck and dodge the heron. She had to tuck Jake under her arm to hold him tight.

The heron could not catch Jake. She had to watch Tim and his mom and dad

and Jake the Snake go inside. The heron lost. She was no match for Tim's mom.

Back inside, Tim's mom said, "We were almost too late. But luck was on our side, Jake." Jake had a scratch on his back, but he was fine. Tim's mom gave Jake to Tim. Tim let Jake stretch out, long and black, in his hands.

"Are you okay?" said Tim.

"Sssafe and sssound," said Jake. "With only a ssslight scratch. Thank you."

Tim's mom cried, "A secret pet snake who speaks!"

"I kept him secret so that you would not make me let him go."

"Well, it made me sick to see the heron peck Jake like that," said Tim's mom.

"Jake, thank you for my wife's ring," said Tim's dad. "And for your work with the mole in our yard. You are a very good pet. We would like you to stay with us. Tim, can Jake stay in your room?"

Tim began to smile and smile. "You mean I can keep Jake?"

"Jake, would you like to live with us?" said Tim's dad.

"Yesss, sssir," hissed Jake. "I would like to live here very much. I would like to be Tim's pet and go with him to school. I would like to go to the beach and watch the sun set. And I would like to read more books."

"You can read!" said Tim's mom.

"Some books," said Jake. "Not a big stack of books. Well, I can read one book. I can read a snake book."

"We have books on snakes and books on moles and books on rings. You can read all the books you like, Jake. And you can eat all the meat you like. You can go to school with Tim and live here with us. We will look after you."

"Thanksss," said Jake. He let Tim hold him tight for a long time.

At the end of the day, a boy and a snake, a mom and a dad, and a cat and a dog all went to the beach. Jake could hitch a ride on Ned's back. They all had to watch the sky for herons that might snatch snakes.

They got to the beach, and Tim's dad made a big stack of beach sand. Tim helped to pack it tight. They made a ridge in the stack of sand, so that all of them could fit on it and sit on it.

Then Tim and his pets and his mom and his dad watched the sun sink into the sea.